PHIL MONROE

The content contained within this book may not be reproduced, duplicated, or transmitted without direct written permission from the author or the publisher.

Under no circumstances will any blame or legal responsibility be held against the publisher, or author, for any damages, reparation, or monetary loss due to the information contained within this book, either directly or indirectly.

Legal Notice:

This book is copyright protected. It is only for personal use. You cannot amend, distribute, sell, use, quote or paraphrase any part, or the content within this book, without the consent of the author or publisher.

Copyright © 2024 by T77 LLC

Disclaimer Notice:

Please note the information contained within this document is for educational and entertainment purposes only. All effort has been executed to present accurate, up to date, reliable, complete information. No warranties of any kind are declared or implied. Readers acknowledge that the author is not engaged in the rendering of legal, financial, medical or professional advice. The content within this book has been derived from various sources. Please consult a licensed professional before attempting any techniques outlined in this book.

By reading this document, the reader agrees that under no circumstances is the author responsible for any losses, direct or indirect, that are incurred as a result of the use of the information contained within this document, including, but not limited to, errors, omissions, or inaccuracies.

Published by: T77 Press

ISBN: 979-8-9909167-0-8 (Hardcover)
ISBN: 979-8-9909167-1-5 (eBook)
ISBN: 979-8-9909167-2-2 (Audiobook)

My Interview Secrets
www.myinterviewsecrets.com

CONTENTS

Introduction vii

Chapter 1.   **How to Sell Your Skills** 1
- Showcase Your Top Five Skills 2
- Tailor Your Skills to the Job Description 3
- Highlight Your Skills in Resumes and Cover Letters 4
- Common Mistakes to Avoid 5
- Present Your Skills Confidently in Interviews . 6

Chapter 2.   **Map Your Skills to the Job Description** 8
- Understand the Job Description 9
- Identify Your Relevant Experience and Skills . . 11
- Use Specific Examples to Demonstrate Your Talents 12

Chapter 3.   **Develop an Experience Story Map** 14
- What Is a Skills Blueprint? 15
- Connect Past Experiences to Future Roles . . . 17
- Use Stories for Maximum Impact 18

Chapter 4. Know Why You're the Best Candidate Ever 21
- Understand Your Unique Value............ 22
- Differentiate Yourself With Past Experiences. 23
- Demonstrate Enthusiasm and Passion 24

Chapter 5. Selling the Close and Connection 27
- Crafting a Compelling Elevator Pitch 28
- The Power of a Simple "Thank You" 29
- Reinforcing Candidacy Through Follow-Up . 31

Chapter 6. Things to Know About the Company 34
- Research the Company 35
- Make an Impression With Company Knowledge............................... 36
- Ask Insightful Company Questions......... 38

Chapter 7. Prepare Your Environment Before an Interview 41
- Check Your Surroundings................. 42
- Test Your Equipment..................... 44
- Make a Good Impression 46

Chapter 8. Practice Your Pivot Before the Question. . .48
- Talking About Your Weaknesses 49
- The STAR Method 50
- Show Resilience and Adaptability During Challenges....................... 52
- Demonstrate Emotional Intelligence........ 53

Chapter 9. **Plan Your Transition Before the Recession** **55**
- Job Transitions in a Changing Job Market . . . 56
- Be Prepared for Unexpected Employment Changes 57
- Build a Strong Professional Network. 59

Chapter 10. **Package and Resell Your Skills in a Competitive Market** **62**
- Create Your Personal Brand 63
- Tailor Your Resume and Cover Letter. 65
- Get Your Stories Ready 67

Conclusion **69**

References **71**

INTRODUCTION

I remember my first interview like it was yesterday. The position was with a government contractor and the interview would take place at a hotel. Walking into the hotel lobby, I felt a mix of excitement and nervousness at the idea of possibly securing my first job. I had no idea what to expect, but I was about to find out that this interview would be unlike any interview I could have imagined. To my surprise, the company had rented out an entire hotel floor! It was bustling with activity, with candidates nervously chatting among themselves and company representatives buzzing around. The atmosphere was filled with anticipation and excitement, and I couldn't help but feel a surge of adrenaline as I waited my turn, even if the setup was akin to speed dating.

Once I sat down for my interview, the questions weren't about my credentials or degree; instead, the questions focused more on how I would respond to different situations. They asked behavioral questions to gauge my reactions and problem-solving skills. It was my first taste of the behavioral interview technique a method widely used by employers to assess your suitability for a role, based on your past behavior in situations relevant to the position. It was a challenging experience, especially with more than 20 other applicants vying for the same position. I did my best, but I wasn't sure how to make myself stand out from the competition, and neither did I know the best way to showcase my skills and personality.

Fast forward to today, and I now sit on the other side of the table. I've made a successful career for myself and transitioned from interviewee to interviewer. Through the ups and downs of changing jobs, dealing with layoffs, and securing promotions, I've learned a thing or two about acing interviews. In this book, I'll share my career journey, successes and failures, and the interview secrets that helped me stand out in a competitive job market. Whether you're a recent graduate looking for your first job or a seasoned professional aiming for a career change, I hope these tips and insights will help you take on your next interview with confidence and skill so that you can land the job of your dreams.

Chapter 1

HOW TO SELL YOUR SKILLS

A job interview is similar to a sales pitch, except you are trying to show a prospective employer that you are the best candidate for the role. It's important to showcase your skills and abilities, but how you present them is even more crucial. I like to focus on my top five skills, and the ones I highlight depend on the role, company, and type of interview. But just like you decide to apply to a job based on the description, a potential employer starts evaluating you before you even arrive for the interview. Their evaluation starts with your resume, making it important to get everything right, from presenting your skills, to using spell check.

SHOWCASE YOUR TOP FIVE SKILLS

Identifying your top five skills is a critical step when you get ready to apply for a job or prepare for an interview. By identifying your top five skills, you can focus on what you are good at and how that makes you an excellent candidate for a role. So what are your top skills? Well, let's figure it out.

Start by developing a skills inventory where you list all your skills. Identify the skills to include by focusing on your strengths and what you know you can do well, be it leadership, communication, organization, or more specialized knowledge like specific programs or expertise. If you're uncertain about your skills, consider asking your friends and family what they believe your strengths are; they might even tell you about a skill that you never considered before. Another unique way to identify your skills is by writing down what activities you do and how you do them on a daily or weekly basis, and identifying skills from there.

Now that you have your skills inventory, identify any themes by grouping similar skills together. This can help you summarize your abilities concisely. Rank your skills with the ones you are best at right at the top of your list. For your top five, start thinking about examples you could use in interviews to demonstrate your proficiency in these skills.

TAILOR YOUR SKILLS TO THE JOB DESCRIPTION

When you read a job description, do you recognize any of your skills that match well with the job? That's exactly what you want because it shows you could be a good fit for the position. It's possible that your top five skills may not be an exact match to the requirements, but that's why you need a personal skills inventory that you can refer to. This way, you can choose your top skills according to the requirements of a job, setting you up as an excellent candidate.

Review the job description carefully to understand the key skills and qualifications desired by the employer. Highlight anything that matches your own strengths and experiences. Compare your skills inventory with the job description and make notes about what your top five skills will be for its application. Take careful note of the language used in the job description because you want to word your skills in a similar way when you get to the next step and prepare your resume.

HIGHLIGHT YOUR SKILLS IN RESUMES AND COVER LETTERS

Now that you have matched your skills to the job description, you need to reflect them well on your resume and in your cover letter. Some people choose to list their skills in a separate section near the top of their resume; that is fine, but you still need to explain them in better detail later on. It might be a better option to have a professional summary in that space where you can mention your skills and how they play into your suitability for a position. Of course, it's always best to use similar language and vocabulary as seen in the job description as it shows you are paying attention and makes it easier for applicant tracking systems a computer program used to help narrow down candidates for a position to process your application.

In your experience section, demonstrate your skills by providing quantifiable examples. For example, if you say one of your top skills is sales, you could mention that you "increased sales by 22%" in a specific role. Here's another example: Instead of mentioning "communication skills," you could say you "improved team communication and efficiency by implementing a new project management system." By providing results, you show potential employers that you can do the necessary work and deliver results.

When it comes to writing a cover letter, you also need to use similar phrasing to the job description and ensure that you describe your top five skills well. It's possible that you may need to complete an online application form, so include all your skills on it too. Use the opening paragraph to introduce yourself and mention the skills you possess that make you a strong candidate for the position. In the body of the cover letter, provide examples of how you've used these skills in previous roles and explain why they make you a good fit for the job. Reiterate your interest in the position and thank the employer for considering your application in the closing paragraph. Sometimes, you won't be asked for a cover letter, but you can still include one by saving it as the front cover of your resume, or by placing it in an "extra information" box in your online application.

COMMON MISTAKES TO AVOID

As you prepare your resume and cover letter, there are a few common mistakes you want to avoid at all costs. One of the most common mistakes is failing to use spell check; ensure your resume and cover letter are free of spelling errors. Microsoft Word and Google Docs both have built-in spell checkers that will also pick up grammar mistakes, but you need to ensure it is set to either UK or US English, depending on where you reside. Additionally, check that your resume is easy to follow and formatted well to help the reader find the information they are looking for quickly. This means using headings that clearly label sections, such as "qualifications" and "experience."

Not tailoring your resume and cover letter is another major mistake, but you can avoid that by following the details in the previous section. However, it's important to be honest in your application, so do not lie or embellish your experience. Instead, focus on sharing relevant experience and information and provide evidence for what you are saying. Explain why your experience is relevant to the position by pointing out the duties you were responsible for and indicating how you went above and beyond what was expected. Avoid mentioning irrelevant skills just to fill up the space on your resume. It's better to stick to a few key skills mentioned in the job description rather than including a bunch of information that doesn't meet the company's requirements.

Sometimes, despite your best efforts, you may notice a mistake on your application after you submit it. That's not the time to pick up on mistakes, so you need to review your resume and cover letter thoroughly before you apply for a position. Ensure your contact details are correct and clearly stipulate what the best way is to reach you. While we are on this topic, the email address you use on your resume should be professional, such as your initials or first name and surname. If you add links to your social media accounts or a portfolio, double-check that they are working and that these accounts reflect you in a positive light. Remember, your potential employer will evaluate you before you even set foot in an interview.

PRESENT YOUR SKILLS CONFIDENTLY IN INTERVIEWS

If you received an invitation to an interview, you are already on track to a potential job offer. Now you need to ace your interview, and if you prepared your resume well, you are already getting there. Review the job description and what you put in your resume and cover letter to recap your top skills. Write down several examples of how you exhibited the skill based on your experience so that they are fresh in your mind and ready when the interviewer asks you about these skills. We'll get into the details on how to answer these and other questions in subsequent chapters.

There are also a few other things to consider when you have an interview, whether it is in-person or online. Arrive at least 10 minutes before the start of your interview. Dress professionally; if you need an idea of what to wear, check the company's social media pages to see how their employees dress for work. And learn as much as you can about the company by doing some research on it.

So, do you have an idea about your top five skills yet? After getting work at one of the biggest semiconductor firms in the world, I was certain that I would stay there until I retired. To my surprise, I was talking to a recruiter within two years, and we were discussing my top five skills during a phone screening.

Chapter 2

MAP YOUR SKILLS TO THE JOB DESCRIPTION

Describe your past (or current) role and main responsibilities. Are you familiar with this interview question? It's one that will definitely be asked in any interview, and how you answer it can make or break your interview. It's not enough to rattle off your job title and responsibilities; potential employers want to ascertain whether you understand the details of a job, how to do it well, and how your experience will apply to your new role. Answering this question well starts with understanding the job description and how you can make your experience more appealing to a potential employer.

UNDERSTAND THE JOB DESCRIPTION

A job description serves two purposes: Firstly, it helps employers define what qualifications, skills, and experience they want in an employee. Secondly, it helps job seekers, like you, determine whether their skills, qualifications, and experience make them good candidates. More importantly, a job description can help you decide if the role aligns with your career goals.

Let's go through the different parts of a job description.

- **Job title:** The job title is the name of the position you're applying for, and quite possibly, the search term you entered while browsing for jobs. It tells you what the role is called and may give you a glimpse into the responsibilities and seniority of the role. For example, it could be "Senior Engineer," "Marketing Intern," "Junior Bookkeeper," or "Administrator."
- **Summary or overview:** Here you will find a brief description of the job which gives you a snapshot of the

key aspects of the role, such as its purpose and the type of work you'll be doing.
- **Responsibilities or duties:** The tasks and activities you'll be expected to perform are listed under the responsibilities or duties section. This part outlines the specific job functions you'll be responsible for on a day-to-day basis and helps you understand the primary focus areas of the role.
- **Requirements:** The requirements section can usually be split into qualifications, experience, and skills required to perform a job successfully. It may stipulate qualification requirements, such as a financial degree to work as an auditor, as well as the number of years of experience needed for the role, such as 10 years of experience to be considered a senior consultant. The requirements may be a combination of these factors too, or in some cases, the company may forgo an official qualification if a person has the relevant experience. This section may also give details about the skills you need to succeed, so look at those carefully.

This is a general idea of what you can expect to see in a job description. Some companies do things a bit differently. For instance, they may explain what a typical day in the role may look like or stipulate what you should be able to do within a week, month, and three months. But even if the job description looks slightly different, you should still be able to identify the basic components. In some cases, the job description may mention the hourly wage or monthly salary as a specific amount or range. This is just an idea of what you may expect to be paid, but usually this is a negotiable number so don't take it as a reason not to apply for the position. The job description may also discuss the culture of the company which can be a great help in deciding whether you will fit in or not.

Something else to consider is that a job description may include specific instructions for the application process. These instructions are given to determine whether candidates can follow directions and pay attention. For example, you may see that you have to answer certain questions, send your application to a specific email address, or complete a task to include with your resume. If you follow the instructions, you are on the right track already because a lot of people do not consider these special requests which may result in their applications being thrown out.

IDENTIFY YOUR RELEVANT EXPERIENCE AND SKILLS

After reading the job description properly, it's now time to link it to your experience and skills, specifically the top five skills you identified in the previous chapter. Open both your resume and the job description so you can see them side-by-side. Go through the job description from the top and match each requirement with something on your resume. It's okay if you don't meet the exact skill or experience needed employers also want to see your enthusiasm for the role but it helps to have some other transferable skill or experience that may be suitable. For example, if the job description lists "organizational skills," your previous experience in administrative tasks can be a suitable substitute or complementary skill. Similarly, if the job description states you need five years of experience, but you only have four years of experience, you should still apply because your enthusiasm, knowledge, and experience could cover all the other requirements in some way. In all likelihood, you already considered these aspects when you applied to the position, but it's good to take note of them for any future applications you do.

Right now, you need to focus on how you can present why you are the best candidate when it is time for your interview. To do so, you are going to do the same thing as described in the previous paragraph, but you need to consider how you will explain them to the interviewer. One way to help you do this is to imagine yourself in the role and completing daily tasks. Think about how you would describe those activities to the interviewer. Pick out some recurring keywords from the job description that you can use during the interview, especially if they are linked to your top five skills. You may need to write them down somewhere to ensure you remember them.

USE SPECIFIC EXAMPLES TO DEMONSTRATE YOUR TALENTS

Let's circle back to that question at the beginning of the chapter: *Describe your past (or current) role and main responsibilities.* This question will be one of the main ones used to demonstrate your abilities and top five skills. Preferably, you want to refer to each of your five skills during the interview as you describe your responsibilities, and the best way to do so is by describing specific examples.

The interviewer should already have seen your resume, so you don't need to list all your qualifications and experience again; instead, focus on specific elements of your resume that link well to your past role and the one you are applying for. Essentially, you want to show that what you've done in the past can help you in a potential job.

Let's say you are applying for a marketing position where one of the responsibilities is email marketing and another is graphic design. You know one of your top skills is copywriting and you have some experience with design too. In your answer, you can describe creating marketing emails, including writing the copy and designing the email as part of your responsibilities. If possible, disclose the results of a specific email campaign, like saying that a particular email campaign for Valentine's Day increased sales by a certain percentage. This is also the ideal time to throw in the names of any specialized software or applications you use in your email marketing process.

By providing specific examples of your skills and matching them to the job description, you are proving to the interviewer that you can do the tasks they described in the job description. It helps them link your experience to the position and gives you a better chance of getting a job offer.

Chapter 3

DEVELOP AN EXPERIENCE STORY MAP

In my role as an engineer, I was expected to construct process maps to demonstrate business activities. A process map is a visual that shows a series of steps or activities involved to complete a specific task or to achieve a goal. It is used to show how these actions will flow from start to finish and includes the sequence, decision points, and interactions between different elements in the process. Usually, these maps are used in business and project management, but they can also be useful in finding and securing a new job. This is where my interview secret comes into the picture! I used the idea of a process map to create a circular flow chart called a skills blueprint to help reposition my career in the marketplace.

WHAT IS A SKILLS BLUEPRINT?

A skills blueprint represents your skills visually, similar to how a process map indicates workflows. It can help you map out your skills and the skills needed for a particular job or career path; this way, you can identify any skills gaps and see how your skills can fit with the job description. A skills blueprint can also help you plan your career development, set goals for acquiring new skills, and make decisions about your education and training.

Have a look at the example of a skills blueprint below. It shows a person's name and job title in the middle. Around that, it shows a specific job responsibility followed by the core skills used in that responsibility. Choose three to five skills for each responsibility. That is followed by another responsibility that links to the previous core skills, and so the circular flow chart continues. The skills for each responsibility can be transferred to another responsibility (in a new role) in some way.

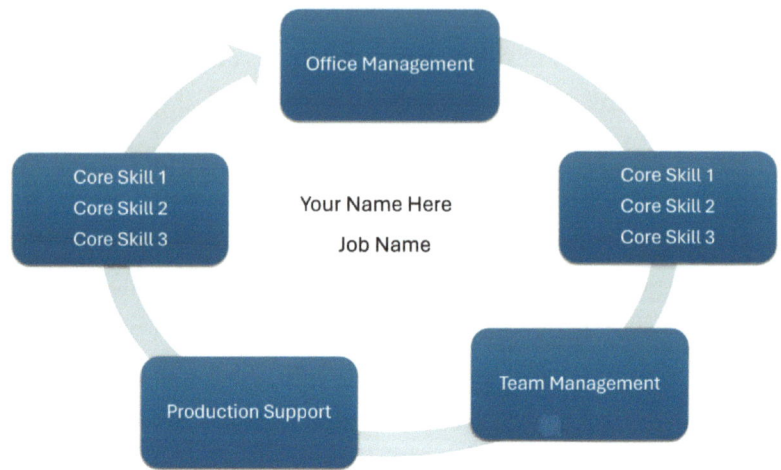

In the example above, one of the job responsibilities was office management. The core skills used in this responsibility could include organization, communication, and decision-making. All of these skills are relevant to team management. Even if the person applying for the position hasn't managed a team directly, they can demonstrate how their skills in office management have gotten them ready for team management.

To adapt the skills blueprint for yourself and the role you applied for, focus on how your current responsibilities have prepared you for new responsibilities. Refer back to your top five skills and how they can be applied to the new role. Take one specific responsibility in the job description and write down your top skills that link to it. Next, think about which current responsibility also has these skills. Link it all together and your skills blueprint should start to take shape.

CONNECT PAST EXPERIENCES TO FUTURE ROLES

With your skills blueprint in hand, it's time to prepare for your interview. You already identified some transferable skills based on your current and potential role, so now you need to link them properly. You can use a similar process to the example in the previous section: Choose a responsibility, figure out the associated skills, and apply them to the new role. If possible, identify a specific event from your past to demonstrate these skills, and do this for each requirement or responsibility stated in the job description.

The more you can tap into your past experience, the more options you have to choose from when you answer questions in your interview. Some questions that may come up include:

- Tell me about a time that you solved a problem.
- Give an example of a time when you had to make a difficult decision with limited information. How did you approach the decision-making process?
- Tell me about a time when you identified an opportunity and took the initiative to address it.
- Describe a situation where you had to negotiate with a colleague, client, or supplier to reach a mutually beneficial agreement. What was your approach? What was the outcome?

As you can see, all of these questions are behavioral. The interviewer wants an answer that shows your thought process, the actions you took, and the outcomes of your actions. It gives them a better idea of whether you will fit in with their organization and have the necessary skills to succeed in the role. But there are many different questions they could ask which is why you need to delve deep and link as much of your prior experience as possible to the future role.

USE STORIES FOR MAXIMUM IMPACT

We've spoken about this quite a bit already, but I need to stress how important it is to use stories when answering questions in an interview. Simply saying that you have "solved problems" is not sufficient; you need to demonstrate this skill with a story from your personal experience. Generally, you can prepare your answers using the following steps:

Identify the responsibility or requirement.

Start by choosing a specific responsibility or requirement for the role; it could be a skill, experience, or quality the employer is looking for in a candidate. Many will be listed, but choose only one to focus on for now.

Reflect on relevant stories.

Think about your past experiences, both professional and personal, that demonstrate your ability to meet the identified responsibility or requirement. Reflect on stories that showcase your skills, accomplishments, and problem-solving abilities. You may want to jot down some notes for each story.

Determine your transferable skills.

Identify the transferable skills you used in each story; preferably, your focus should be on your top five skills. Your transferable skills should be ones that can be applied to a variety of roles and industries, such as communication, teamwork, and leadership. Write down the skills that are relevant to each story.

Choose one story that demonstrates your skills best.

Select one story that you believe best demonstrates your skills and aligns with the responsibilities and requirements of the new role. Focus on a story that has a clear beginning, middle, and end, and highlights your abilities in a positive light. Essentially, you want to explain the situation or problem, what you did to solve it, and the outcome.

Align the story with the employer's needs.

Now that you've chosen a story, tailor it to align with the specific needs of the employer and the job. Highlight how your skills and experiences make you a strong fit for the role and how you can contribute to the success of the organization. This is a great time to review the vocabulary used in the job description. Determine how you can use some of the recurring keywords in your story.

Add enough details without losing your focus.

Provide enough detail in your story to give the interviewer a clear understanding of the situation, your actions, and the results you achieved. You can focus on specific processes, collaborative efforts, and methods you used during that time. However, be mindful of not including irrelevant details that could detract from your main points. The best way to do this is to write down your story. Do several iterations and ask yourself whether each bit adds value or if it's unnecessary. Continue doing this until you are happy with your story.

Ask if the interviewer has any questions.

After sharing your story, ask the interviewer if they have any questions or if there's anything else they would like you to elaborate on. This shows you value their input and want to engage them in conversation.

Remember, preparing stories for an interview will take time, but it will also set you apart because the interviewer will pick up on your preparation. As you prepare your stories, you'll probably realize that a single story can demonstrate several of the responsibilities mentioned in the job description. Focus on a few core skills to discuss in the story while still adding some details that cover other responsibilities or requirements. Keep the stories you don't use in your pocket for other questions or use them to demonstrate your ability in other parts of the job description.

The skills blueprint made all the difference in my professional life. After I presented it to the hiring manager and discussed my skills, I was able to secure a new job and received a $10,000 salary increase because I proved myself as a proficient specialist. The skills blueprint will help solidify your position against equally qualified candidates because it's a tool to help demonstrate why you are the best option. Take some time now to create a skills blueprint for yourself based on a job you want to apply for.

Chapter 4

KNOW WHY YOU'RE THE BEST CANDIDATE EVER

I can never forget one specific morning meeting. It was filled with an unnerving silence. We all waited nervously for the CEO to announce the news although many of us already knew what it would be that the company was downsizing. The reality of what was to come was a shock to us all, even if we had anticipated it to some extent. A sense of panic was palpable. It was as if someone had swung open a door to a devastatingly unknown future.

As I looked around the room, I realized I was one of the lucky ones. I had been with the company long enough to build relationships, had proven myself time and again, and earned the respect of my colleagues and leadership. But still, I was being asked to leave. Determined to make the most of the situation, I took what I had learned and started looking for opportunities where I could apply my skills in different areas, both inside and outside of the tech industry. I had loads of experience in developing applications, but instead of focusing only on that, I decided to consider other skills I had gained, including leadership, problem-solving, and communication.

UNDERSTAND YOUR UNIQUE VALUE

You already know you can bring some kind of value to a new role, but what is that value? You have to do a deep dive into both your current role and the broader skills you've acquired to help you find your unique value. Begin by reflecting on your current role and consider the skills and experiences that have contributed to your success. Think about the challenges you've overcome, the accomplishments you're proud of, and the impact you've had on your team or organization.

In the previous chapter, we discussed how transferable skills may be relevant to a future role. This is the time to think about those transferable skills and how they can be applied to different contexts and industries. Determine what sets you apart from other candidates. It could be your personality, your approach to challenges, or your perspective on work and life.

Ask for feedback from colleagues, mentors, or supervisors to get their insight into how they perceive your strengths and areas for development. You might find that they say something you didn't recognize in yourself. For example, if you work in customer service, a coworker might point out that you ask customers a lot of questions to ensure you understand their situation. You may identify this as active listening and inquisitiveness which are essential if you were to apply for a role as a manager. Remember to tailor your value proposition to align with the specific needs of the role you are interested in and applying for; this will make you stand out even more.

DIFFERENTIATE YOURSELF WITH PAST EXPERIENCES

Being unique helps you to differentiate yourself, and the best way to do this is by tapping into your past experiences. In the previous chapter, we discussed how you can use stories for maximum impact, but you need to choose these stories carefully. The experiences you tell an interviewer about should set you apart from the competition, so they don't want to hear generic stories that could happen to anyone in any role. Here's a basic example: If you are applying for an entry-level role and get the question, "What is your greatest achievement?" interviewers don't want to hear that it was graduating with your degree. They may expect all applicants to have a degree anyway so it doesn't set you apart. Interviewers would prefer to hear about a project you took part in that had outstanding results.

Focus on showcasing your achievements and the impact you've made in previous roles. Instead of just listing your job duties, highlight specific accomplishments and challenges you've overcome. Describe the situations you faced, the actions you took, and the results you achieved. Think about the skills and qualities that helped you succeed in these situations. Giving concrete examples of your past experiences demonstrates your capabilities and helps you stand out as a strong candidate.

After the initial upset of losing my job, I found a new job and moved on into several different roles. I was applying my experience to all sorts of settings and positions. I learned to think on my feet and to find solutions to complex problems. The more experience I gained, the more I started to see how I could use my skills to help others, like you, who are struggling to navigate the corporate world. I want you to stand out! When I finally returned to the tech industry, I had developed a better understanding of my value and how to stand out. I was no longer just another job candidate; I was someone who could bring something unique to the table.

DEMONSTRATE ENTHUSIASM AND PASSION

Have you ever felt excited about a specific role after reading the job description? It's the kind of excitement that makes you believe a role was made for you. That's an amazing feeling! You want the interviewer to pick up on your excitement.

During your interview, express your enthusiasm for the role and the company. Mention some of their projects that appeal to you and where you know your skill set can be valuable. Talk about why you're excited about the opportunity and how your skills and experiences make you a great fit. Share specific examples from your past that demonstrate your passion for the industry or field. Ask thoughtful questions about the role, the team, and the company to show your interest and engagement. Illustrate your knowledge of the industry by sharing insights or ideas that showcase your passion and commitment to making a positive impact in the role.

Speak with enthusiasm about your abilities, and tell the interviewer about the skills and qualities that you're the proudest of and that have contributed to success in your career. Show excitement about the opportunity and the chance to apply your skills in new ways while continuously developing them. Talk about how you're always looking for ways to grow and improve your skills. The key is to be authentic and genuine in your enthusiasm for the role, your skills, and your abilities. When you're passionate about what you do, it's infectious, and it can help you stand out as a candidate.

Pay attention to your body language during the interview. Non-verbal cues, such as the way you sit, your gestures, and your posture, all convey your feelings about a role and the interviewer's question. Your body language can speak volumes about your passion and enthusiasm for a role. A genuine smile can show you are excited about the opportunity and happy to be there. Maintain good eye contact to show you are engaged and interested in the conversation; it also conveys confidence. Sit or stand up straight with your shoulders back for an extra boost of confidence and to demonstrate you are participating actively.

Hand gestures and facial expressions also convey your enthusiasm. Gestures can help emphasize your points; however, it's important to use gestures that are natural and not overexaggerated, as that can be distracting. Your facial expressions should also match the words you are saying or flow with the conversation. For example, nodding your head while listening can show you are paying attention to what is being said. When you speak, keep a lively tone and appropriate volume that conveys enthusiasm. Avoid speaking too softly or monotonously as it can make you seem disinterested. Speak clearly and at a pace that is easy to follow.

In the end, I was grateful for all the experience I gained after losing my job. The journey was challenging, but it made me a stronger, more capable professional and allowed me to develop many other skills. The company I left gave me a chance to see that it was possible to survive a recession, and come out on the other side with greater knowledge and a better understanding of what it takes to be successful in any field.

Chapter 5

SELLING THE CLOSE AND CONNECTION

Interviews can be short or long, but one thing is undeniable: A lot of information is shared. Most of that is information about you, and by the end of the interview, it may be slightly challenging to remember exactly what was said at the start. That's why it's important to do something different that will leave a lasting impression on the interviewer. For me, this boils down to three things: First, summarizing your potential using an elevator pitch; second, thanking the interviewer for their time; and finally, following up after the interview. These are simple actions but they can go a long way and help you stand out from other candidates.

CRAFTING A COMPELLING ELEVATOR PITCH

An elevator pitch is a short, convincing statement that is meant to persuade someone of something in this case, to offer you a job. The idea is to leave a strong, lasting impression about why you are the best candidate for the role. This final moment should succinctly describe your key strengths and resonate with your potential employer long after the meeting ends. It should highlight your top skills and reinforce why you are the right fit for the job. It should also be short enough to add at the end of the interview without making the meeting run over time. You can say your elevator pitch if the interviewer asks if you have anything else to add or right before saying goodbye.

Begin by identifying the top two skills you want your interviewer to remember. The two you choose should be based on the top five skills you identified previously and be directly relevant to the role you're applying for. They should also align with the company's values or objectives.

Clearly state the two core skills you excel in. Make sure these skills have been discussed previously during your interview so they are familiar to the interviewer rather than new information. You can also offer a quick snippet of how you've successfully applied these skills in real-world scenarios, but keep it brief. For instance, if you are applying for a marketing role, you could say, "Throughout my career, my ability to think creatively has led to innovative campaigns that drove a 20% increase in customer engagement." Make sure you connect the dots between your skills and the role in question. Explain how your capabilities and experience will benefit their organization specifically. For example, you might adjust your elevator pitch to, "I believe my creative problem-solving and analytical approach could bring fresh insights to your upcoming product launch, ensuring it reaches the target demographic effectively." This kind of statement shows you understand the job responsibilities and have looked into the company as well.

Remember to keep it brief about 30 seconds to a minute. Focus on clarity and conciseness. It's always a good idea to write down your elevator pitch so that you can memorize it more easily. Practice your elevator speech until it flows naturally, without sounding rehearsed. Use any opportunity you get to rehearse your elevator pitch, such as saying it to yourself in front of the mirror or to family members.

THE POWER OF A SIMPLE "THANK YOU"

In my experience, the simple act of saying "thank you" at the end of your interview can leave a positive and lasting impression on your potential employer.

Thanking the interviewer shows you have good manners, but it also speaks volumes about your character. A "thank you" sends a clear message that you appreciate the opportunity the interviewer has given you to showcase your skills, discuss your experience, and talk about a future with the organization's team. Acknowledging this opportunity can highlight your understanding and respect for the hiring process, which, in turn, reflects positively on you.

When you show appreciation, you set yourself apart from the competition. Hiring managers often see many applicants, and amidst many interviews, someone who takes a moment to express sincere thanks stands out. It's a subtle but memorable way to distinguish yourself.

A simple "thank you" helps you connect on a human level. Interviews are filled with technical discussions about qualifications, experiences, and future roles, which can make the whole process cold and repetitive. However, a "thank you" creates a personal connection and reminds the interviewer there is someone behind the resume and skill set. It shows you are a person who values courtesy and human decency. This is really important when you work in teams because getting along well with others can make a big difference in the success of the team. By expressing gratitude, you set the tone for a respectful working relationship.

Expressing gratitude also provides closure to the interview and wraps up the conversation on a positive note. The interviewer leaves the meeting feeling appreciated, which may influence their memory of you. Think back to some conversations you've had in the past, whether during an interview or other setting. Most likely, conversations that you remember fondly are the ones that were polite, whereas negative conversations may have occurred when the other person was rude or lacked basic manners. The same goes for your interview, and the interviewer will remember your gratitude. Ensure the final moments of your interview are marked by thoughtful appreciation to leave the interviewer with a favorable impression.

To truly maximize the effectiveness of your "thank you," consider personalizing it. Instead of a generic expression, tailor your thanks to the specific context of the interview. Mention something particular you discussed or an aspect of the company that excites you. For instance, if you learned about an innovative project during your discussion, express your appreciation for being told about it and share why it genuinely interests you. Personal touches show that you were engaged and attentive throughout the interview. Just remember that sincerity is key. Empty gestures can be picked up on and potentially harm rather than help your cause. Ensure that your thanks are genuine and reflective of your true feelings about the opportunity and the interaction.

REINFORCING CANDIDACY THROUGH FOLLOW-UP

After you've wrapped up your job interview, you aren't done quite yet. While it's normal to wait a few days before hearing back from the interviewer, that does not mean they shouldn't hear from you. Following up can be an important part of reinforcing why you are a good candidate and leaving a good impression. It's an opportunity to demonstrate your follow-up abilities, remind the employer of your strong points, and keep yourself top-of-mind as they make a decision.

Employers appreciate candidates who show initiative and gratitude. A well-crafted follow-up message can often be the difference between getting the job or not. It shows that you are proactive, respectful, and genuinely interested in the role. It also shows that you won't sit back if you are given the job and a task is delayed because the interviewer will know you already have the skills and tenacity to follow up and get things back on track.

Start by sending a thank-you email within 24 hours of your interview. It demonstrates courtesy and appreciation for the interviewer's time. Keep it short and sweet, but make sure to reiterate your enthusiasm for the role. Mention specific points from the interview to personalize it or how the organization's values align with your own. For example, if the interviewer mentioned a particular project you'd be working on, express how excited you are about that prospect, or if they mention the different departments that you will be working with, you can mention how it will be useful to get insights from other areas outside your own.

Use the follow-up opportunity to succinctly recap why you're the best fit for the position by emphasizing the key skills you bring to the table and how they align with the needs of the company. This isn't the time for a lengthy novel keep it to one or two sentences, but make them count. Be direct but friendly. You can use a variation of your elevator pitch to help craft your email. Make it clear that you remain interested in the role. Sometimes, despite a great interview, the hiring manager needs reassurance that you're still keen, especially if they saw additional candidates after your interview. You might say something like, "I am even more enthusiastic about joining your team after our conversation."

You may also be wondering when you will hear back from the interviewer or what the next steps are in the process. If the interviewer didn't provide a timeline for their decision-making process, it's perfectly appropriate to inquire politely about the next steps in your follow-up email. Doing so helps you manage your expectations and reduces any anxiety about the wait. A simple line such as, "Could you kindly share when I might expect to hear back?" will suffice. Even if you get a response back saying that you haven't been successful, your follow-up email will have provided a sense of closure. But then again, a follow-up email might be exactly the push an interviewer needs to make you an offer!

Chapter 6

THINGS TO KNOW ABOUT THE COMPANY

A surefire way to impress an interviewer is to have knowledge about the company, and yet, many candidates don't make the effort. I love the reaction I get from the interviewer when I share facts about the company, its CEO, and the major projects they are working on in that quarter. Knowing about a company shows you understand the details and demonstrates a willingness to go the extra mile.

RESEARCH THE COMPANY

There are many reasons to do some research about the company. Of course, you want to know about them and how they work, but it also shows your genuine interest in the position. Hiring managers can pick up your company knowledge and that immediately sets you apart from other candidates. Doing research communicates dedication, enthusiasm, and a proactive approach which are all qualities highly valued by employers.

Learning more about the company can make your decision-making process easier. You want to find a workplace where you'll thrive instead of merely getting a salary and benefits. For instance, your values and working style need to align with those of the organization. By delving into what the company stands for and how it operates, you can better assess if it's a place where you'll be happy and productive in the long run.

Even though the company's website is a good start, it's important to explore various aspects of the company, and that may require some other sources of information. Start with its website to get a feel for its mission statement, core values, and services or products. Pay attention to the language and tone used on the site; it often reflects the company's culture and priorities. Have a look at recent news articles, press releases, and social media channels that provide insights into the company's current trajectory, challenges, and achievements. Platforms like Glassdoor and LinkedIn are invaluable for gathering insider perspectives because they offer employee reviews and testimonials, revealing details about the workplace environment, management style, and overall employee satisfaction.

When you walk into an interview with detailed knowledge about the company, you portray confidence and competence. You can also include some of your company knowledge in your responses without being asked about the company directly. For example, if the interviewer asks why you want to work there, you can reference a recent project or achievement of the company that resonates with you to make your answer more personal and compelling. Using company knowledge helps you contribute to a dialogue about how your skills and experiences align with the company's goals instead of providing standard answers.

MAKE AN IMPRESSION WITH COMPANY KNOWLEDGE

Before your interview, spend some time on the company's website to learn more about it. At a minimum, you need to review the company's core products and services, the number of employees, the most recent quarter's earning report, and the name and tenure of the CEO. Memorize as many facts as possible and incorporate them into your answers when the interviewer asks what you know about the company.

Start by visiting the company's website, especially the "Products" or "Services" section to learn more about what the business does. Industry reports or news articles can give insights, while customer reviews or testimonials may help you understand how these products or services are perceived.

The "About Us" or "Corporate Information" section on the company's website can reveal details about the workforce. Check for information about the number of employees and different office locations. Are they a local start-up with a close-knit team, or a multinational giant with offices around the globe? Does the company allow for hybrid or remote work? Understanding the company's size and structure can help you gauge the work culture and potential career growth opportunities. Bringing up an office location during your interview might even show that you've considered the logistics of commuting or relocation, demonstrating foresight and commitment. Additionally, you may find details about the CEO which can help you understand their leadership style and vision.

It's important to review the most recent quarter's earnings report as it contains valuable insights into the company's financial health and strategic direction. This step is crucial because it shows that you care about the company's future as much as your own. You should find the report under the "Investor Relations" section on the company's website. Sometimes, these reports include other relevant information like the number of employees, current or prior projects, and sales volumes. Discussing these reports during your interview can position you as someone who understands business. Make your conversation more substantive and engaging by mentioning specific figures or trends.

Finally, look at the company's mission, vision, and values to see how yours aligns with theirs. It will help you determine if you're the right fit for the company and give you talking points that resonate on a more personal level. These details are found in the "About Us" section, or sometimes, it has its own page called "Mission and Values." When your values align with the company's, it makes it easier to fit in. For example, you could mention that you are particularly drawn to the company's commitment to sustainability and innovation as these are values you are passionate about. If possible, add in an example of how you've practiced these values in the past.

ASK INSIGHTFUL COMPANY QUESTIONS

During your interview, you should have the opportunity to ask questions. It depends on the interviewer, but you will be able to ask questions throughout the interview or at the end. If you've done your research, these questions should come easily and be integrated well into your conversation. Being inquisitive about the company shows you did your homework and look forward to being a part of the team; that can make you stand out from other candidates.

Asking informed questions serves many purposes. By asking well-researched questions, you show that you've invested time in understanding the company which is something any employer would find appealing. Thoughtful questions help build rapport and create deeper conversations that help you connect better with the interviewer which may make you more memorable. Understanding the company's structure, expectations, and culture can help clarify if you will thrive in that environment. Your questions can help you figure out if the company's values and goals align with yours. A mutual fit is important for long-term satisfaction and success; otherwise, you may get the job only to realize that you don't work in the same way as your colleagues. It's a two-way street; as much as the company evaluates your fit, you should assess theirs, too.

Prepare your questions based on your research ahead of your interview. For example, if you read about a recent product launch, ask about how they identified the gap in the market, the process that went into creating the product, or how it has been received by customers. While having questions prepared is a good start, stay open to organic discussion, because sometimes, the conversation may lead to unexpected avenues that offer more valuable insights. Find a balance between asking for information about the company's operations and expressing your passion for the role. The questions you ask should be relevant to your prospective responsibilities and experience.

Here are some examples of questions:

- I saw that your company recently launched a new AI-driven product. Can you tell me more about the role the marketing team played in that launch and the strategies that were most effective?
- I noticed that innovation is one of your core values, and I'm really passionate about driving innovative technology strategies. Could you share an example of how team members here have leveraged creativity in their efforts?
- With the rapid growth trajectory that the company is on, what opportunities for professional development and career advancement can employees expect?

These kinds of questions encourage engaging and thoughtful conversation while also helping you learn more about both the company's operations and your potential fit within it.

Do not underestimate the power of thorough company research. It's easy to assume that showcasing your skills and experience will be enough to impress your interviewers but failing to understand the company's background can leave you at a disadvantage even if you are the most qualified candidate. Interviewers ask behavioral questions and you can too. Think about it from the interviewer's perspective: One candidate only talks about their own achievements, while the other candidate mentions specific company initiatives, aligns their answers with the company's values, and asks questions about recent developments. The second candidate clearly stands out because they are qualified, dedicated, and can think strategically. Which candidate do you want to be?

Chapter 7

PREPARE YOUR ENVIRONMENT BEFORE AN INTERVIEW

Have you seen some screen recordings from virtual meetings where something goes wrong? I've seen videos of people not realizing they have a cat filter on them, people using a background of a beach, and people dressed professionally until they stand up for some reason and reveal their shorts. That's not what you want to happen in your interview and with video meetings becoming more popular, you need to ensure you are ready for them. Companies are increasingly transitioning to a remote or hybrid work model, so the probability of having a video interview is high, but you also want to be genuine, just like you would be in person. Recently, we experienced an incident where the candidate did very well in the video call, but when we invited them to the office, it wasn't the same person. You don't want that to happen to you, so let's talk about how to make your video interview successful.

CHECK YOUR SURROUNDINGS

Where will you be when you have your video interview? It's something to think about, especially if you do not have a dedicated home office space. You want to come across as professional and that starts with being aware of your surroundings and background.

The space behind you should be clean and free from distractions because a cluttered or busy background can divert attention away from your conversation and inadvertently send the wrong message about your organizational skills. Try to find a neutral wall or a tidy corner in your home where you won't be disturbed. It might mean setting up a temporary desk somewhere or removing decor from the wall, but it's worth it to leave a good impression. It's fine if you have a plant or appropriate picture in the background, as long as you believe it will give a professional experience. If a neutral wall isn't a possibility, virtual backgrounds can be a useful alternative as long as they are professional and not too distracting. Choose something with a solid color; depending on the platform, you may even find backgrounds that look like an office.

How you sit is also an important consideration. You need to be comfortable, but that does not mean lounging in a chair or on your bed. Instead, use a supportive chair that encourages good posture, as this can significantly how you are perceived. Sit up straight like you would if the interview had been in person. While you are finding a good way to sit, also check your camera. Position it at eye level to avoid awkward angles and to ensure it feels more like a face-to-face conversation. Looking directly into the camera while speaking can create a sense of eye contact, which helps build rapport and shows confidence. If you struggle to look at the camera, there are some computer programs you can download that help you focus on the camera.

Part of getting your surroundings ready is ensuring sufficient lighting while you are having the meeting. Good lighting can significantly enhance your appearance on camera and ensure that the interviewer can see you clearly. Natural light is an excellent option, so if possible, position yourself facing a window but check that the light isn't so harsh that it makes you look pale. However, avoid having a window directly behind you as it can create a silhouette effect, preventing the interviewer from seeing you properly. If natural light isn't an option, consider using a lamp or an LED ring light. Adjust the height and position of the light until your face is well-lit without harsh shadows or glares.

Something else to consider is background noise. Ambient sounds, like traffic, dogs barking, and alarms going off, can be incredibly disruptive during an interview. Choose a quiet area in your home where you are less likely to be disturbed by household members, pets, or street noise. If possible, close the door to the room you will be in. If other people will be home during your meeting, let them know about your important interview, and that you would appreciate their cooperation in keeping the noise level down. Even better, ask them to leave the house for a while, and encourage them to take any noisy pets with them. Alternatively, consider using headphones with a built-in microphone as they can help minimize ambient noise and ensure your voice comes through clearly.

TEST YOUR EQUIPMENT

As you prepare your space for the interview, you also need to make time to test your equipment. The last thing you want is to be midway through an interview only to have your equipment fail, or even worse, struggle to connect to the meeting from the start. Testing can help you avoid these issues.

Start by considering your internet connection, as stable internet is essential to have a smooth video interview. It's important to have a stable and fast internet connection to prevent lag or disconnections, which can be disruptive and unprofessional. Run a speed test several times in the days running up to the interview to ensure your line is suitable. If your Wi-Fi is unreliable, consider using an Ethernet cable for a direct connection to your router which can significantly improve your internet stability. Additionally, disconnect any other devices before your meeting to help decrease the internet load.

Next, test your audio equipment, including your speakers and microphone. Poor audio and microphone quality can frustrate both you and the interviewer which may lead to miscommunications or being misheard. Test your microphone to ensure it works properly and delivers clear sound. Make sure your voice comes through clearly without any distortion or interruptions. Headphones with a built-in mic can often provide better audio quality than your computer's default settings.

Setting up and testing your camera is just as important because the interviewer needs to see you clearly. Your facial expressions can communicate a lot about you so you want a clear image. Test your camera to confirm that it displays a clear picture and make the necessary adjustments something as simple as wiping the lens can make a big difference. Position your camera at eye level. It may be necessary to place your screen or laptop on a stack of books to help elevate it to the right height. Reposition the camera until it shows your entire face and shoulders, and center yourself in the frame for a professional appearance.

As you work on your setup, familiarize yourself with the video conferencing platform you'll be using. Make sure you know how to join the meeting, mute and unmute yourself, and share your screen if necessary. All of these things demonstrate technical competence, preparedness, and reliability. It may also be useful to conduct a mock interview with a friend or family member to check that everything works well. A practice run will help you identify any potential issues and give you time to fix them so that everything runs smoothly during your interview.

It's best to plan for a worst-case scenario, and that includes having a backup plan in case something goes wrong with your setup or you experience a technical glitch. If your computer freezes or your internet drops suddenly, having a phone number to call or an alternate method to reconnect can save the interview. Inform the interviewer beforehand that you're prepared with a backup plan and ask them if there is anything you need to know to help get the interview going again. Besides being a good idea, it also shows foresight and adaptability. If you are using a laptop, connect it to a power source during your interview as you don't want the laptop to shut down and disrupt the meeting.

Check your computer for any updates as they can take a while to download and install and may cause your computer to be slow or lag; you want to avoid this happening during your interview. Additionally, open up your task manager or activity monitor and close any unnecessary applications running in the background as they can consume valuable bandwidth and processing power. You only want the video platform open while you are doing your interview.

MAKE A GOOD IMPRESSION

The same standards expected of you in an in-person interview apply to a video interview. You should still dress professionally as it sets the tone and conveys your seriousness about the opportunity. If you attended an in-person interview, you would arrive a few minutes early; the same goes for virtual meetings. Log into the video platform a few minutes earlier than the scheduled time to show you are punctual. It also gives you a buffer to address any last-minute technical issues should any arise. Use the time until the interviewer joins to take a few deep breaths and calm any pre-interview nerves.

Body language is important. Maintain good posture by sitting up straight, try to avoid fidgeting, and do not cross your arms over your chest. Make eye contact by looking at the camera rather than at the screen. It can feel a bit awkward because that means you aren't looking into the eyes of the interviewer but it will present you correctly on the interviewer's screen. This small adjustment can create a sense of connection and attentiveness. Smiling and nodding occasionally can also help in making the interaction feel more personal and engaging.

No matter how diligent your preparations are, the unexpected can still happen. Do not stress if something goes wrong. Maintain your composure under technical difficulties to show your resiliency and problem-solving skills which are qualities employers are looking for anyway. If things go wrong despite your best efforts, communicate it swiftly and calmly to the interviewer. A brief apology and a clear explanation of the issue along with your immediate plan to rectify the situation can indicate you keep your cool under pressure.

Chapter 8

PRACTICE YOUR PIVOT BEFORE THE QUESTION

One of the questions most candidates find unnerving is "What are your weaknesses?" or "Tell me about a time you made a mistake." These questions aren't created in an attempt to catch you out; they are simply assessing your behavior and self-awareness when you are faced with a challenge. When asked about something I need to improve, I like to find the middle ground and explain how I'm handling the situation differently now. This way, I can provide precise details about challenging scenarios and explain how I can apply the lessons I've learned in my upcoming endeavors.

TALKING ABOUT YOUR WEAKNESSES

There's no need to panic when an interviewer asks about your weaknesses, failures, or mistakes. With the right approach, you can turn what seems like a difficult question into an opportunity to shine and demonstrate your growth mindset. It's important to be honest yet strategic. You want to prepare your answer in a set format so that the question doesn't catch you off guard. It requires acknowledging a genuine area of weakness and explaining why this particular area has been challenging for you. Next, discuss the steps you've taken to address and improve upon this weakness and highlight what you've learned from this process. Essentially, your answer should illustrate how it contributes to your professional growth.

For example, suppose you struggle with public speaking. You could say, "One area I've been working on is my public speaking skills. In the past, I found myself getting nervous when presenting to larger audiences. To overcome this, I took a public speaking course and volunteered to do some more presentations at work. Through these experiences, I've gained more confidence and improved my ability to communicate effectively which has taught me the importance of continuous self-improvement and resilience."

By structuring your answer this way, you acknowledge a real weakness and showcase your commitment to growth and learning. It's a balanced approach that helps interviewers see your potential and dedication to personal development rather than focusing only on the weakness itself. When you address areas of improvement, you signal that you have self-awareness. Employers want to know that their employees are aware of their limitations and willing and able to take deliberate actions to improve.

As you discuss areas for growth, frame them as opportunities for skill enhancement. For example, if you identify time management as an area for improvement, explain how you're actively seeking ways to better manage your workload. Perhaps you could mention using project management software or time-blocking techniques, and how these tools have helped you prioritize tasks and meet deadlines consistently. Answering questions this way reassures the interviewer that you won't shy away from difficulties but instead face them head-on. Remember to express your enthusiasm for learning too, as employers appreciate candidates who want to expand their skill sets.

THE STAR METHOD

We've already gone over the basic way to answer questions about your weaknesses, and the STAR method situation, task, action, result can make it even easier. This method can showcase your competencies and experiences in a way that's both compelling and clear-cut. The STAR method offers a structured way to present your stories and makes it easier for interviewers to follow and assess your qualifications. More importantly, it ensures you discuss all critical aspects of your past experiences. This method can also be used to answer other behavioral questions during your interview.

Follow these steps to prepare your response:

- Situation: Think about a specific event from your past experiences where you played a significant role. Help the interviewer visualize the context by explaining the situation concisely. Choose a situation that relates to the job description and demonstrates the skills you may need in it.
- Task: Next, explain what you were responsible for. Discuss your specific duties within the scenario you just outlined. For example, you were tasked with leading a project, overcoming a particular challenge, or meeting an ambitious goal. Use this time to clearly define your role and the expectations placed upon you.
- Action: Explain the steps you took to address the task. Add sufficient detail about your process, but keep your explanation streamlined. The interviewer wants to understand your thought process without getting lost in minutiae.
- Result: Wrap up your answer by describing the outcome of your actions. If possible, quantify your success as numbers provide concrete evidence of your impact. For example, "After I started using project management tools, my productivity increased by 25%."

The STAR method is a great way to prepare your responses, especially if you know you will be discussing your weaknesses or areas for improvement, but remember to remain honest. The interviewer isn't expecting you to be perfect; they want to see that you can take action when things aren't going according to plan. Be confident, yet humble. If other people were involved in helping you to solve the problem, acknowledge their efforts. Emphasizing your ability to collaborate with colleagues to find a solution shows you are a team player. After all, personal achievement often occurs due to collective effort.

SHOW RESILIENCE AND ADAPTABILITY DURING CHALLENGES

Employers know that things don't always go according to plan, so interviewers want to see your ability to demonstrate resilience and adaptability particularly in difficult situations during your interview. If you can show that you have the grit to face challenges head-on and the flexibility to adjust your approach as needed, you'll differentiate yourself from other candidates.

Resilience shows the interviewer that you don't break down under pressure and you bounce back after setbacks and keep going. Sometimes, interviewers will ask you about a time you were resilient. Select a story of when things didn't go as planned at your previous job but do not dwell too much on the problem rather talk about how you responded. For example, you could mention you organized a quick team meeting to brainstorm solutions, or you stayed late to get things back on track.

You should also touch on adaptability when discussing your weaknesses and areas for improvement. Adaptability means you can change your ideas when needed and aren't stuck in rigid ways of thinking or working. Employers want to know that if the industry changes or your role evolves, you can keep up. To demonstrate adaptability, share an anecdote where you had to adapt to new circumstances, such as when the company underwent a major technological change, or there was a sudden shift in market demands, and you had to learn new skills or adopt new strategies rapidly.

Saying you are resilient and adaptable is not enough. You have to provide proof of this to the interviewer by giving them concrete examples. The evidence you present needs to be specific and relevant to the company and job description. Do not be vague in your answer; it's best to give specific details about the situation and the actions you took.

DEMONSTRATE EMOTIONAL INTELLIGENCE

Most of the time, your weaknesses and areas for improvement will come out in performance reviews, so you can include suitable anecdotes during your interview. The interviewer wants to know that you can make improvements based on the feedback of others, especially management and team members. When you receive constructive criticism, do you take it on board and use it to enhance your performance, or do you become defensive? Explain to the interviewer how you handled feedback constructively in the past, as it speaks volumes about your character and willingness to grow.

Emotional intelligence is just as important as technical skills, and your prospective employer will keep that in mind. Being able to manage your emotions and understand those of others is important, especially in high-pressure environments. If you've ever been in a situation where tensions ran high perhaps during a tight deadline or a significant organizational change and you helped calm the storm, this is something worth mentioning. It's not a problem if you can't recall a specific scenario as your emotional intelligence will still shine through in your other answers and stories.

It's more important to communicate how emotionally loaded experiences have prepared you for the role you're applying for. Tailor your anecdotes to reflect some of the responsibilities outlined in the job description. For instance, if the position requires managing diverse teams, discuss times you've flourished in multicultural settings or led teams with varied skill sets. If the role involves quick decision-making, present scenarios where your prompt and effective decisions turned adverse situations around.

As you move forward, consider every interview question about weaknesses or areas for improvement as an opportunity to reflect on your career progression and articulate your readiness to keep growing. In doing so, you'll enhance your chances of succeeding in interviews and pave the way for a fulfilling career where you can succeed daily.

Chapter 9

PLAN YOUR TRANSITION BEFORE THE RECESSION

The days of working for one company for 40 years and then retiring are no longer the norm, especially in the IT field. The organization's management, culture, and economic factors can lead to leaving a job within three to seven years. For that reason, you need to stay ahead of the curve and be prepared for anything. It doesn't mean you should sit back you can still give your current role your all and be a great performer. But it's also smart to stay in touch with recruiters and look out for potential positions, just in case something unexpected happens when you get to work on Monday.

JOB TRANSITIONS IN A CHANGING JOB MARKET

Every few years, the economy becomes unstable and people start talking about a potential recession. The harsh reality is that economic downturns often lead to downsizing, budget cuts, and restructuring within companies. For example, during the last recession, many professionals found themselves caught off guard and scrambled to update their resumes at the last minute. Doing so can be particularly worrisome if you've been with an employer for many years and haven't kept your resume updated. Unpreparedness can result in stress, longer periods of unemployment, and missed opportunities so the secret is to be prepared for anything.

It's not as simple as finding a new position. A job transition is about aligning your career trajectory with your personal aspirations and market demands. It's important to recognize that this may take time and you may experience setbacks, but with a robust plan and a proactive approach, you can turn these challenges into opportunities. You want to focus on career progression as well as your well-being. Even if you are ambitious, a career change can be stressful and emotionally taxing so you need to be kind to yourself. Facing job loss or significant career changes can be daunting and stressful. However, having a backup plan can reduce some of this anxiety. This is also where resilience comes into the picture, as it will help you cope with the immediate changes and equip you with the mental toughness to do well in a new role.

While you consider new opportunities or a backup plan, consider the broader perspective. A new role or industry may not look like what you imagined initially. Stay open to the idea that your career path may contain lateral moves or even temporary steps back instead of an upward trajectory but that may be necessary for greater progress. It's the perfect time to diversify your experiences and skill set which may open doors to unexpected opportunities.

BE PREPARED FOR UNEXPECTED EMPLOYMENT CHANGES

When you looked for a new job, long before your current one was in question, you undoubtedly did a lot of preparation. Right now, you need to do the same thing, even if you aren't worried about your job. Your backup plan hinges on preparation.

Start by assessing your current skills and do a skills inventory as explained in earlier chapters. Identify your transferable skills as well as those requiring some improvement. You can use these skills to draft a resume that you can tailor to different positions. While you are busy with that, update your resume to reflect your most recent experiences and achievements.

Since you are thinking about your future, you may also want to reflect on your long-term career goals. Where do you see yourself in five to ten years? What roles and responsibilities excite you? Is your current position helping you work toward these goals? A clear career path can help you identify the roles you want to be in and how they will move you toward securing your dream job. Take some time to set specific, achievable milestones for your career. You may find that your ideal career path reveals some missing skills or qualifications, so come up with a plan to help you bridge those gaps in the meantime. The power of ongoing education cannot be overstated, so consider enrolling in courses or earning certifications that enhance your expertise. Many top universities and institutions offer affordable online programs some are even free that can fit into your busy schedule.

Staying relevant in your field is equally important. With rapid technological advancements and evolving industry standards, continuous learning and adaptation are non-negotiable. Subscribe to newsletters, follow thought leaders on social media, and read relevant publications to stay informed about the latest trends; you will also be able to use this knowledge in potential interviews which may give you a competitive edge. Use your newfound knowledge in practical settings by taking on freelance projects, volunteering, or collaborating with colleagues. These experiences will sharpen your skills and indicate your commitment to growth and excellence.

With your career plan and industry knowledge in hand, it's time to research potential employers and even alternative industries. Check company websites for hiring opportunities or contact them directly to find out about potential roles. Sending your resume to a recruitment agent and having an initial conversation with them can also connect you to emerging opportunities that align with your skill set and values.

Think about it from the perspective of a potential employer: When another company undergoes restructuring or downsizing, employees who have anticipated changes and prepared accordingly tend to fare better. If this is you, then you already have a polished resume, a LinkedIn profile that reflects your current skills, and a network of contacts you can reach out to. You aren't caught off guard because you've laid the groundwork for potential transitions whether they are planned or unexpected. Additionally, companies appreciate individuals who demonstrate foresight and initiative. When you show that you've taken steps to prepare for various career outcomes, it signifies you're responsible and forward-thinking. Preparing this way positions you as someone who doesn't wait for situations to dictate actions but rather takes charge of your career outcomes.

BUILD A STRONG PROFESSIONAL NETWORK

There is one timeless element that can provide stability and open doors throughout your career journey: a strong professional network. A robust network creates meaningful connections with people who can offer support, guidance, and opportunities when you need them most. We'll talk about how to build a network in a minute, but keep in mind that you should focus on quality connections rather than having many superficial contacts. Focus on quality interactions, and gradually, your network will become a reliable source filled with opportunities and support.

To build your network, you need to engage with others. Begin your networking by attending industry conferences, local meet-ups, or seminars related to your field. These opportunities could be in person or online, so make the most of it and participate to let other people know you are here. Reach out, introduce yourself, and follow your greeting with thoughtful questions about their work. When you meet someone new, focus on building a mutually beneficial relationship. What can you offer them? Maybe it's sharing an interesting article, providing feedback on a project, or introducing them to another valuable contact. As in any relationship, give more than you take, and the returns will follow. After the event, follow up with new contacts by sending personalized messages expressing your appreciation for their time and insights. Connect with them on professional social media platforms like LinkedIn where you can share your thoughts on current trends, comment on others' posts, and celebrate their achievements. If possible, organize informal meet-ups, get-togethers, or discussion groups within your community or workplace to strengthen your existing connections and attract new ones.

Your network can be a great help if you are looking for a new position, so let people in your network know that you are open to work. Often, job opportunities come through word-of-mouth and personal recommendations. By networking, you increase your chances of being considered for roles that align with your experience, skills, and interests. Reach out to several of your contacts for informational interviews about the companies they work at or roles you're interested in. These conversations can provide you with valuable information, help you understand the company's culture, and potentially lead to job openings before they're publicly advertised. How you ask for potential opportunities matters too so be clear about what kind of role you're looking for and where your skills lie.

The job market changes constantly, and it's possible that you may be secure in your position today but be worried about your role tomorrow. It helps to prepare for these possibilities. And remember, if you face hard times, seeking help can be a strategic move towards resilience. Utilize resources like career counseling, peer support groups, and online forums to find guidance and motivation during challenging times.

Chapter 10

PACKAGE AND RESELL YOUR SKILLS IN A COMPETITIVE MARKET

In most companies, a large team works together, but that can be daunting and it makes it difficult to stand out among the rest. However, the experiences you gain from your roles and being part of a team are what make you unique. Prospective employers can easily fill a position by looking for someone with the right credentials, but it's your experiences that differentiate you. Throughout this book, we've discussed how stories can demonstrate how you excelled in specific areas, the importance of tailoring your resume for a role, and the power of an elevator pitch. Let's bring it all together and get you ready to shine in your interview.

CREATE YOUR PERSONAL BRAND

One of the most empowering steps you can take as you prepare for a new job opportunity or an upcoming interview is to create a personal brand that showcases your experiences and skills. Your personal brand represents what you do: It's who you are, what you stand for, and how you want others to perceive you in a professional setting.

To develop your personal brand, do some self-reflection. Take some time to think about yourself as a professional. What accomplishments define your career? What unique skills do you bring to the table? More importantly, what values and principles guide your work ethic? Identify these core elements to help you lay the foundation of your personal brand.

Once you've identified your strengths and values, you need to present them consistently in person, on paper, and on digital platforms. Think about your resume, LinkedIn profile, and even your personal social media accounts. Are they telling the same story? Does each platform reflect your unique value proposition? Will prospective employers see the same person and characteristics if they look at your TikTok account versus your resume? Consistency is important because employers may check multiple sources to get a holistic view of you. Ensure that every piece of information reinforces the narrative you're crafting and makes you proud of who you are.

To create a streamlined brand, conduct a thorough audit of your online presence and remove any content that doesn't align with the image you want to portray. Next, update your LinkedIn profile to highlight your key experiences, skills, and achievements succinctly. Write a headline that explains what you do or aspire to, and upload a professional photo. Use the same keywords from your resume to make your profile easier to find, and if possible, get connections to endorse some of your skills to help prove your abilities. Use your elevator pitch to write a summary that captures the essence of who you are professionally. Make it concise and memorable. Finally, engage with connections and content that is relevant to your field. You can share articles, comment on posts, and join professional groups to demonstrate your industry engagement.

In addition to curating your online presence, you may want to develop a personal website or portfolio. A personal website gives you an opportunity to showcase your projects, portfolio, and testimonials from colleagues and clients. It acts as a central hub where potential employers can get an in-depth look at your professional life, especially if you include a link to your website in your cover letter, resume, and social media profiles. Plus, a website allows you to control the narrative entirely without the constraints of third-party platforms.

While building your brand, remember that the goal is to highlight the best aspects of who you are and persuade people of your authenticity. Strive to find a balance between confidence with humility, and professionalism with reliability. Remember, your personal brand is dynamic and will evolve as you grow in your career. Update your online profiles and website frequently and ensure they reflect industry trends to help keep your brand relevant and compelling.

As you establish and grow your brand, you may need feedback to ensure you are on the right track. Ask for feedback from peers, mentors, and even interviewers to help you understand how your brand is perceived by them. Use the insights they share to refine your brand and adapt it as necessary to reflect your growing expertise and evolving career goals.

TAILOR YOUR RESUME AND COVER LETTER

The importance of tailoring your resume and cover letter has been discussed before, but I can't stress enough how important this is. To secure an interview, you first have to convince a company that you are worth their time, and that's done with your resume and cover letter. Essentially, your application documents convey your personality and give a potential employer a first glimpse at who you are. So yes, it is worth your time to tailor your resume and cover letter.

Start your resume with a clear objective or summary statement. It should be a concise paragraph at the top of your resume that captures who you are, what you offer, and what you're looking for, so it's quite similar to your elevator pitch. For instance, if you're applying to a healthcare organization, emphasize your dedication to human welfare alongside your professional skills. Next, ensure that your work experience section is focused on achievements by including concrete responsibilities and compelling results. If you were responsible for implementing a new software system that increased efficiency by 20%, say so. It's these specifics that give employers a tangible sense of your capabilities. Beyond your resume's content, its format also matters. A clean, modern design that is easy to read will naturally draw the eye. Avoid overly complicated layouts and stick to standard fonts and bullet points because less can indeed be more.

When it comes to your cover letter, approach it as an unparalleled opportunity to convey your personality, values, and commitment to the role you're applying for. While your resume lists the "what" of your career, the cover letter explains the "why." Start off strong by directly addressing the hiring manager if their name is available; this small personal touch shows that you've done your homework and are genuinely interested. But if you do opt for this more personal approach, you need to review the hiring manager's social media profile and other information to ensure you know more about them for the interview.

Use the first few sentences of your cover letter to capture the reader's attention. You could share a brief anecdote that relates to the company's mission or the role. It immediately creates a personal connection to the broader organizational goals and shows empathy and alignment in values. Move on to describing your applicable skills and experiences but don't reiterate your resume; instead, focus on your top five skills and expand on them with context and storytelling. Show how your past roles have prepared you to contribute uniquely to the new position. End your cover letter with a compelling closing statement that reinforces your enthusiasm and includes a call to action such as expressing a desire to further discuss how you can contribute to the company's success in an interview.

Remember that both your resume and cover letter should contain similar language as in the job posting. Many companies use Applicant Tracking Systems (ATS) to filter through resumes, so a human won't see your application unless it passes through this system. Matching your keywords to those in the job description ensures your application makes it through to a human. However, keywords should be incorporated naturally so that they resonate with the reader while also making it through the technological sieve.

Remain positive as you prepare your materials because even though the process can be tiresome, every tailored resume and personalized cover letter brings you one step closer to finding a better role. With these tools in place, you'll be better equipped to package and resell your skills effectively in any competitive market.

GET YOUR STORIES READY

I've previously mentioned that using real-life stories from your personal experiences can help you do well in an interview. Stories and anecdotes bring a human touch to your professional background and transform it from a list of accomplishments into a living, breathing testament to who you are and what you can do. When told well, your stories will make you memorable and highlight your key skills and attributes.

Which of your stories have already come to mind as you've read this book? Think back to that time when you had to lead a project with a challenging deadline and managed to surpass expectations. Or that instance when you turned a failing initiative into a success by leveraging a unique skill set. These anecdotes offer tangible proof of your abilities and character while portraying skills such as problem-solving, leadership, resilience, and adaptability. If you want to make your stories impactful, focus on situations where you faced a challenge and overcame it. Explain how you used specific skills to generate positive results and include any lessons you learned along the way. These stories can be added to your resume, cover letter, and interview conversations as long as they fit in with the discussion.

In the end, perfecting your personal brand, creating a strong resume and cover letter, and using stories to demonstrate your skills can increase your chances of securing an interview. Keep refining your story, be open to feedback, and maintain an optimistic outlook. Each step you take brings you closer to realizing your true potential, even if it takes some repetition. Keep going, your next interview is right around the corner!

CONCLUSION

Thinking back to that initial meeting with the government contractor, I clearly recall how they evaluated my credentials and aptitude, but more than that, they were ascertaining whether my character was a suitable match for their organization. The same may happen in your interview. Every business has its strategies, processes, and culture which guide executives, managers, and general staff to collaborate and execute tasks successfully, and this will flow into their interview methods too. Once you understand these aspects and align them with your skill set and narrative, it makes it easier to pursue a position because it will become more obvious whether the role and company are a good fit for you.

You will ace the interview when you articulate the abilities listed on your resume, demonstrate your skills with a blueprint, and back it up with stories about your experience. Make yourself the top choice by concisely summarizing your top five talents and experiences, and you'll leave the interviewer in no doubt that you are the best person for the job.

Best of luck for your upcoming interview! I'm sure my interview secrets will help prepare you to find the job of your dreams.

Remember, your success is determined by the effort, time, and dedication you put into preparing for your next job interview. What are you waiting for? The future is at your fingertips!

REFERENCES

Birt, J. (2023a, March 11). *How to answer "Describe your current job responsibilities."* Indeed Career Guide. https://www.indeed.com/career-advice/interviewing/describe-your-current-job-responsibilities

Birt, J. (2023b, March 11). *How to thank someone for an interview (10 email tips).* Indeed. https://www.indeed.com/career-advice/interviewing/how-to-thank-someone-for-an-interview

Boogaard, K. (2024, May 14). *The STAR method: The secret to acing your next job interview.* The Muse. https://www.themuse.com/advice/star-interview-method

Council post: 14 steps to take to build a strong professional network. (2022, November 30). Forbes. https://www.forbes.com/sites/forbescoachescouncil/2022/11/30/14-steps-to-take-to-build-a-strong-professional-network/?sh=7948d33e755d

Doyle, A. (2022, December 3). *Best answers for what is your greatest weakness with examples.* The Balance. https://www.thebalancemoney.com/what-is-your-greatest-weakness-2061288

Doyle, A. (2024, May 3). *How to create an elevator pitch (with examples)*. The Balance. https://www.thebalancemoney.com/elevator-speech-examples-and-writing-tips-2061976

Falcon, S., & Wiens, K. (2022, July 5). *Reeling from a sudden job loss? Here's how to start healing*. Harvard Business Review. https://hbr.org/2022/07/reeling-from-a-sudden-job-loss-heres-how-to-start-healing

5 ways to find out what your strengths are. (n.d.). Barclays Life Skills. https://barclayslifeskills.com/i-want-to-choose-my-next-step/school/5-ways-to-find-out-what-you-re-good-at/

Forsey, C. (2024, April 23). *7 amazing sample answers to "What makes you unique?"* HubSpot. https://blog.hubspot.com/marketing/what-makes-you-unique

Gordon, K. (2022, November 7). *3 ways to leverage past experience into a new career*. Athabasca University. https://www.athabascau.ca/news/professional-development/3-ways-to-leverage-past-experience-into-a-new-career-2

How can you use storytelling to connect your past experiences to future goals? (n.d.). LinkedIn. https://www.linkedin.com/advice/0/how-can-you-use-storytelling-connect-your-past-experiences

How to identify your skills. (n.d.). Totaljobs. https://www.totaljobs.com/advice/how-to-identify-your-skills

How to make a good impression in a virtual job interview. (n.d.). Handshake. https://joinhandshake.com/blog/students/how-to-make-a-good-impression-in-a-virtual-job-interview/

How to research a company for a job interview. (2024, January 4). Purdue Global. https://www.purdueglobal.edu/blog/careers/research-company-job-interview/

Jones, R. (2022, January 24). *How following up can help you land the job*. The Muse. https://www.themuse.com/advice/how-following-up-can-help-you-land-the-job

Kimbrough, K. (2022, March 29). *A skills-first blueprint for better job outcomes*. LinkedIn Economic Graph. https://economicgraph.linkedin.com/blog/a-skills-first-blueprint-for-better-job-outcomes

Kurtuy, A. (2023, December 27). *How to ace interviews with the STAR method [9+ examples]*. Novorésumé. https://novoresume.com/career-blog/interview-star-method

Laker, B., Godley, W., Kudret, S., & Trehan, R. (2021, March 9). *4 tips to nail a virtual job interview*. Harvard Business Review. https://hbr.org/2021/03/4-tips-to-nail-a-virtual-job-interview

Leveraging networking for job search success. (2024, March 19). Not Monkeys Recruitment. https://notmonkeysrecruitment.com/leveraging-networking-for-job-search-success/

Liu, J. (2023, March 6). *Navigating career transitions: How to change your path one step at A time*. Forbes. https://www.forbes.com/sites/josephliu/2023/03/06/navigating-career-transitions-how-to-change-your-path-one-step-at-a-time/?sh=4207d5747755

Lowe-MacAuley, K. (n.d.). *How to read job descriptions and what to look for*. FlexJobs. https://www.flexjobs.com/blog/post/how-to-read-job-descriptions/

Markman, A. (2020, November 5). *4 ways to follow up after a job interview*. Harvard Business Review. https://hbr.org/2020/11/4-ways-to-follow-up-after-a-job-interview

Orduña, N. (2022, September 28). *How to build your personal brand at work*. Harvard Business Review. https://hbr.org/2022/09/how-to-build-your-personal-brand-at-work

Payne, R. (2021, October 19). *Remote interview tips: 5 tactics to ace your job interview*. Remote. https://remote.com/blog/remote-job-interview-tips

Scherer, H. (n.d.). *10 ways to improve your life after unexpected job loss*. Holly Scherer. https://www.hollyscherer.com/job-loss/

Schwartzberg, J. (2023a, May 2). *How to answer "What are your strengths and weaknesses?"* Harvard Business Review. https://hbr.org/2023/05/how-to-answer-what-are-your-strengths-and-weaknesses

Schwartzberg, J. (2023b, August 22). *How to make your resume match the job description*. Harvard Business Review. https://hbr.org/2023/08/how-to-make-your-resume-match-the-job-description

16 resume mistakes and how to avoid them. (2023, January 3). Indeed Career Guide. https://www.indeed.com/career-advice/resumes-cover-letters/15-resume-mistakes-to-avoid

Sjoerdsma, D. (2021, August 27). *15 steps to align your skills with the job description*. AACSB. https://www.aacsb.edu/insights/articles/2021/08/15-steps-to-align-you-skills-with-the-job-description

Smith, J. (2023, May). *Top 7 CV mistakes.* Prospects. https://www.prospects.ac.uk/careers-advice/cvs-and-cover-letters/top-7-cv-mistakes

Zhang, L. (2020, June 19). *The ultimate guide to researching a company pre-interview.* The Muse. https://www.themuse.com/advice/the-ultimate-guide-to-researching-a-company-preinterview

www.ingramcontent.com/pod-product-compliance
Lightning Source LLC
Chambersburg PA
CBHW041457010526
44119CB00023B/381/J